WORKING THE SCRAPBOOK

WORKING THE SCRAPBOOK

PETER BLAND

All rights reserved. No part of this work covered by the copyright herein may be reproduced or used in any means – graphic, electronic, or mechanical, including copying, recording, taping, or information storage and retrieval systems – without written permission of the publisher.

Printed by imprintdigital
Upton Pyne, Exeter
www.digital.imprint.co.uk

Typesetting, cover design and cover photo by narrator
www.narrator.me.uk
info@narrator.me.uk
033 022 300 39

Published by Shoestring Press
19 Devonshire Avenue, Beeston, Nottingham, NG9 1BS
(0115) 925 1827
www.shoestringpress.co.uk

First published 2017
© Copyright: Peter Bland

© Author photo copyright:
John Schroeder, www.thedigitaldarkroom.co.nz

The moral right of the author has been asserted.

ISBN 978-1-910323-88-5

ACKNOWLEDGEMENTS

Thanks to the editors of the following publications where some of these poems first appeared: *The Rialto*, *The London Magazine*, *PN Review*, *The Times Literary Supplement*, *The Spectator*, and *The Australian Literary Journal*.

For
Karen, Joanna and Carl

CONTENTS

Working the Scrapbook	1
Smile Please!	2
Losing Touch	3
Art Deco	4
The Pond	5
The Parade	7
Exotic	8
The Building	9
At Kensal Green Cemetery	10
At Aldeburgh	11
Tidal Fields – Chidham	12
Something of an Apology	13
Driving Home	14
Bear Dance	15
Mortality	17
More Bits for the Scrapbook	19
The Philosopher	20
Viewing Primitives	21
Staring Time in the Face	22
The Idea of Home	23
The Walking Dead	24
I'm Talking My Way into a Poem Again	26
X-ray	27
Pavements	28
The General	29
This Way to Samarkand	31
On Government Lawns	32
Scarecrow	33
Flâneur	34
Beyond	35
Wilderness Moments in Orange County	36
Overheard in Malibu	37
Travelling West	38
Homage to Hopper	39
The Golden Parrots of Orange County	40
Shopping with Brigitte Bardot	41

A Cold Day in Assisi	42
Barcelona	43
The 1929 Essex Six	45
The Deserted Border	46
Déjà Vu	47
LOSS	49
1. Loss	51
2. Angry	52
3. Outrage	53
4. Clearing Out	54
5. Habits of a Lifetime	55
6. Fugue	56
7. The Piano	57
8. Trinkets	58
9. Elemental	59
10. Other Times, Other Places	60
11. Letting Light in	61
12. I'll Be Waiting	62
13. Poppies	63
14. Cold	64
15. Ashes	65
16. Click	66
17. Stalker	67
18. Didn't I Say?	68
19. There You Are	69

WORKING THE SCRAPBOOK

Nothing's planned: photos, kids' scribbles,
philosophical 'sayings', daily kitsch,
they're all here, part of an ongoing story
with the self hogging centre-stage, but not
as much as I thought it would. It's
the we…you…who…they…of what's happening
with holiday glimpses of a shared 'beyond'
that brings me running to keep it going
even knowing it's of no interest except
to bored family members and well-mannered friends
embarrassed to discover they've almost vanished
under pictures of steam trains, old *Lilliput* nudes,
and menus from another immigrant ship. But
those stuck here can't know what a blessing
their presence truly is. Among
these mementos of what's been and gone
I've put together a tribal thriller,
a paean to trivia, a taut page-turner
where no one can guess what's coming next.

SMILE PLEASE!

Photos travel back. That's
their job. So here I am
on Scarborough sands
being pushed through the '30s
in a second-hand pram. Not
far away, on Castle Hill,
crowded tombstones lose their names
while leaning into a north-east wind.
Even so, the dead seem to know
that as long as we dream them up
they'll be back. Uncles,
aunts, out-of-work dads…
in this pause between wars
they're hanging on,
pulling up bootstraps, tightening belts,
their thin children in the summer light
already ghosting as the cameras click.

LOSING TOUCH

More sunken battleships and abandoned tanks
rusting among old childhood ponds.
Seventy years on I should have wandered
far beyond such troubled scenes. Hey ho,
here they come, the wartime dead…
Mum, Dad, Brother Bill,
but lately they fail to recognize
the child who's become a bald old man.
They've even begun to forget themselves,
drifting back across those childhood ponds
and beyond the great doors of dawn and dusk.

ART DECO

A thirties idyll, something bright and cheerful
to jazz up damp distempered walls....
I remember best a metal yacht on the mantle
safely sailing through poverty and wars.
Won at a whist-drive it was stamped 'Pure Silver'
but turned out to be nickel-plated chrome.

Our 40-watt bulb, wartime shaded,
gave its deck a delicate rosy glow.
'Tahitian red,' mum said, always naming
places she would feel at home.
One by one – mum, dad, sailor brothers –
the family slipped quietly overboard.

When it berthed at the salerooms in '49
that gleaming con-job had outsailed them all.

THE POND

There he is again, that boy, parking his bike
under a hawthorn tree and crawling out through
the reeds to the deepest end of the pond. He's
been coming here every day, arriving just as I
cast my own line into the shadows under the old
willow tree. I like having the pond to myself.
It goes a long way back in my life. I'm over eighty
and the past isn't a mere flicker of old insights,
it actually fosters the illusion of a lost self.
So I'm not totally surprised when this lad keeps
turning up. He's obviously familiar with the place.
I can make out a box of worms, a slice of bread
and cheese, and a bottle of dandelion and burdock.
They bring back sweet memories, the warm fizz of
that summery drink, the moist tang of the cheddar,
with an added bite of raw onion. He's still in
his grey school uniform and his shoes are alarmingly
down-at-heel. He occasionally glances in my direction,
as if sensing there's someone here, but he quickly
turns away. His future is still not firm enough to
be seen.
    It's a beautiful day. It always is. Dragonflies
skim through the shallows, fish mouth the still
waters. There was once another pond in the next field,
but it dropped into a disused coalmine,
– taking a couple of cows with it. Now there's only a
deep muddy hole in the ground. Nothing lasts. Not even ponds.
    The boy's looking up again, shading his eyes.
The pond is a shimmering green surface full of drowned
silences, little trails of fish-fins and insects running
on water. There's the faint hum of bees. The pond is the
entrance to another world. I wait and watch. My little
red float bobs next to some lily-pads. I'd like to live here
forever among crusted cowpats, bee-drone, tree-smells,
pond shimmer.

The plop of my float has settled into a thrilling stillness. What dark shapes are nosing their way in silence towards my baited hook? The tip of my float lets the whole day gather round it.

The boy is staring at me again, as though he finally catches a glimpse of my presence. When I leave at the first chill of dusk, he'll sense my absence, as I will his. Only a lifetime keeps us apart.

THE PARADE

Tonight all my childhood
goodbyes are gathering
through factory smoke
and bombed provincial
streets: father, mother,
war-drowned brother,
if I thought they
could hear me I'd buy
them a drink. But I'm
always so small
as they pass me by
like a travelling circus
leaving town. I used
to cry 'Wait for me!
Wait for me!' But now
I'm at peace and wave
them on. I believe
there's a pact between
the dead and the living
that knows how to share
a lonely road. These
days, as they fade,
family clowns fart
loudly, and the lovely
ladies on their big
white horses
pretend to know me
and lean down
to smile.

EXOTIC

Angela Ackroyd was exotic
back in the '50s. At 15
she painted sexy seams
on her drab school stockings.
Wonder Woman and Tarzan's
Jane were exotic, and
anything Eastern, anything
that tasted like Turkish Delight
and of a paradise where
you never got caned
or were made to sing GOD
SAVE THE KING at the end
of the film. Foreign
stamps were exotic,
especially those with palms
and lots of Lawrence
of Arabias on camels. Even
the poppy Dad wore once a year
was exotic. It was like
a scarlet butterfly
that landed on his lapel
and stayed there all day. You
couldn't take your eyes off it!

THE BUILDING...

seems to have collapsed around me. It could be a bombed-out council house, a deserted air-raid shelter, or an abandoned railway station? Without being able to pin things down I get the feeling of a previously shared history. And why not? One senses that the entire universe is local.

There's a stain on the walls that's more than weathering. One suspects a bad dream left over from childhood, or the sort of splattering a flattened bullet might make after passing through flesh and blood continuously down the years.

The corridors have no ends or beginnings (as far as one can see) and the furniture – bed, table, desk, chairs – is fairly featureless stuff, evading any style or period. Mind you, the bed is made, so *someone* cares, someone among the yellowing photographs of husbands in blood-stained uniforms, of exhausted mothers and wives.

Then there's the scent. Time itself perhaps? Or simply stale polish and long-dead flowers? Through memory gaps and cracks in the floorboards there are constant glimpses of oblivion. Thank god for the sound of the sea, for distant fog-horns and passing breezes, for these thin shafts of sunlight through the boarded-up windows. Only gravity could keep me here. I'm building a small boat from the furniture.

AT KENSAL GREEN CEMETERY

No joke, this weight of stone, these
gothic monoliths with granite scrolls –
clerics and Raj-men, Victorian bosses
in tombs as magnificent as their homes.
Good neighbours all (one race and blood)
secure in their Englishness even in death –
poets no one ever reads, generals
who'll never relax their grip.
                                      And these
in an open patch of earth
next to the main road, far
from sheltering trees – Mr Rajneesh,
Calypso Pete, Harry the Greek, Armenian Joe,
with wedding photos in plastic bags
and flowers in cans among gravel chips
that rattle like seeds as lorries pass.

AT ALDEBURGH

For Herbert Lomas

It's the intimacy that appeals
even here on the beach
where the sea so delicately
licks our feet, moving heaps
of pebbles back and forth

although, occasionally, you warn
it floods the path
between *Ye Olde Tea Shoppe*
and that Martello Tower
they hire out by the month.

That risk apart (and what's a storm
between a poet and his buttered scones?)
it's a landscape that seems so sure of itself
with a sense of tradition
my mind lacks. I envy you

your place here…at home
between engrossed extremes:
the sea, going nowhere where you'd rather be,
and those little lanes through summer fields
that lose themselves as they move inland.

TIDAL FIELDS – CHIDHAM

This is no landscape for a tidy mind,
the sea insinuates, trundling mud
into our inland barn. All night,
though attic-high, we've heard
salt waters lapping underground.
A vision of the flood, you smile,
common after love. Our
bodies flow, our tongues lick salt.
How you love this place where earth
and water meet, where doves
and gannets mingle in the trees
and loaves and fishes populate the fields.

SOMETHING OF AN APOLOGY

    for Beryl

From modest, even grim beginnings
– two-up, two-down, a tin
bath in the kitchen – I dreamt
of living in old water-mills,
a sun-drenched vicarage, barely
habitable abbeys.
                Beguiled
by old notions of nature's grace,
I acquired a thwarted sense of belonging
and passed this on to those I love.
(Not a drab inheritance but one
frayed with panic.) Forgive
the restlessness I landed you with,
the worn-out shoes, the childhood baggage,
the lonely campfires, the ruined follies.

DRIVING HOME

Tell me you're waiting
at three in the morning
in your best silk dress
and that your skin
smells of spring. Tell me
the children are sleeping
and the dark is listening
silently for my key
in the door. Tell me
it will always be this way
and that time passing
will bring us together
again and again. Tell me
of love and love's
miraculous greetings.
Tell me you're waiting,
knowing I'm almost there.

BEAR DANCE

for Beryl

To bring you to my bed
I dramatize myself:
I walk through the house
in primary colours.

How else can I be seen
among all the children and flowers
among all the music and mirrors
among all the open windows
that surround us?

I have to shout
to wear bright shirts
to dance up and down
rattling the cups in the kitchen.

The children laugh.
They say I'm a bear.
They like it best when I roll on the ground.
They say there's a dancing bear in the house.

But this is my love dance.
Ahee…I bellow
before clicking my tongue
like the starlings in the early morning
when they think they've swallowed the sun.

This, I say, is my love dance.
With this I'll bring you to my bed
again and again.

When you see me in my bright shirt,
when you hear neighbours and friends complaining
saying I'm loud and heavy-footed,
remember that my dance is for you.
It's in your sole honour.
It has to compete with your silence
and with the other silences that go on and on
like the sky through these open windows
forever....

MORTALITY

*Terrible to give back this soul
which acted as if it had got used to me*
– Jacques Reda

The reality of it
first entered in
on a railway bridge
when I was 10
and I saw my own body
through wreaths of steam
becoming nothing
in a hole in the ground.

I howled in panic.
It was so unfair!
This only happened
to cats and dogs
and people far off
I'd never met.

Then it happened
to Mum and Dad
to friends in fast cars
and wartime brothers
to grey-haired uncles
and a lifelong lover.

It was a disease.
It was a summons.
It was a coiled snake
in the pit of my stomach,
But I learned its name,
I absorbed its presence.
This kundalini
was my own dark essence.

I carry it with me
night and day
as it eats
its own tail,
as we watch
and wait.

MORE BITS FOR THE SCRAPBOOK

Different times, places,
people, things. As Einstein said
'all points in time
somehow co-exist.' I'm
putting this to the test
and placing events
in no particular order. That's
half the fun. Now that,
now this. It's strange
how the dead
never seem lonely. That's
a legacy they've left
with us. In page
after page times co-exist
because that's how I've *not*
arranged them. The dead
and the living both
look up and grin.

THE PHILOSOPHER

I met an old man begging in the street and put a small coin in his hat. He stared at me with wild blue eyes, grabbed my sleeve, and did his Ancient Mariner bit. 'The facts, man, the facts of our being here. Truth and beauty guv. We didn't ask to be here but, bugger me, the mysteries keep mounting up.' I agreed. Encouraged, he rambled on. 'Infinity is in the scent of a flower guv. Didn't Blake say that?' Not quite, I replied, but I get your drift. 'Fuck me, guv, I know god's immeasurably other, but I need the bus-fare home.' I put a bigger coin in his hat. 'It's all in the moment guv, remember that. It has to be. Nothing else makes sense. Every alternative is in the moment. Shit, I've made some bad choices over the years.'

I turned to go, but he pulled me back. 'You're a good man guv,' he intoned. I felt embarrassed. 'No, no,' he mumbled. 'I mean it. You can always tell a person's essence by the allowances he makes.' I'm not making any allowances, I assured him, I just happened to be passing and I'm interested in what you have to say. He pulled me closer. His breath was a sewer. 'It's important to feed the soul,' he confided, 'but I'm dying for the want of a Big Mac.' I slipped a further few coins into his hat. Then he unscrewed a bottle of cheap sherry and offered me a sip. Having already smelled his breath and glimpsed the matted contour of his tongue, I declined, again turning to leave. 'Concerning our origins,' he shouted after me, 'there was always something before there was something. There was never nothing. So don't believe them when they say there was.' I won't, I yelled back. 'Promise,' he insisted. Don't worry, I promise.

At the corner of the street I decided to look back. He was talking to a solid-looking middle-aged woman and gripping her shopping trolley. 'Beauty is truth luv,' he was saying with great tenderness, while kissing her large outstretched hand. 'See if I care,' she hissed, kicking him quickly in the balls before hurrying off.

VIEWING PRIMITIVES

In the best work nothing's willed:
everyone shares a sense of occasion
and the proper self-esteem. People
seem to be in fancy dress (wedding groups,
clean children, minor government officials)
but this is simple reportage...
though God knows where it could lead.

As witness one scene where Rousseau picks up
some solitary leaves. These
tempt him to visit the botanical gardens
where jungles are suddenly commonplace
and where his neighbour's unattainable nude wife
can be safely arranged on a studio couch
among artistic tigers and edible flowers.

STARING TIME IN THE FACE

On the bedside table there's a glass of iced water
(the invisible made solid) and a shimmer of dust
on my little blue pill.

Your side of the bed's less anxious
with its perfumes, bangles, vanishing creams
(although you're still here) and that deco-clock

worn out by all the wars, steam-trains,
old immigrant boats, and lives it's lost.
Why do we keep it now it's stopped?

I snuggle up close and take my pill,
waiting patiently for love to happen
watched by a clock that's chucked it in.

THE IDEA OF HOME

One has to admire its persistence.
The way it follows us around
ignoring borders and demanding more
than a cave, a tree-bed, a hole
in the ground. Is there no end
to its ambitions? Where did
we get this trust in four walls?
Even now, going global
and on the move, we dream
of a future with many mansions
and a smooth infinity of heavenly lawns.

THE WALKING DEAD

The only way to kill zombies is to blow their brains out. Otherwise, as we know, they'll live forever and feed on human flesh. Like vampires and other creatures of the dark, they have a terrifying taste for human blood. But recent research has shown that while humans are increasing at an alarming rate, zombies are becoming quite rare. They are a dying breed, hunted to extinction by humans with an ever-increasing need to blow out brains. Following their retreat into isolated rural areas, zombies are often mistaken for mythical creatures called 'Bigfoot' when glimpsed in thick forests. As far as we can tell no one has been eaten by a zombie for some years, and the well-known zombie specialist Dr Felix Bland (no relation) has successfully lived with a group of forest zombies for some years without being attacked. He reports radical changes in their behaviour and has even begun a small breeding programme, following his discovery that one or two advanced females of the species had taken to mating with reclusive mountain men in Alberta. The resulting offspring show a distinct improvement in their motor-neuron balance, and one cross-breed has even learned to play the piano, using two fingers and the occasional elbow. For some unexplained reason Dr Bland reports that forest zombies find early French baroque music (Lully and Rameau in particular) extremely calming. One has even been known to attempt a clumsy gavotte. When isolated from humanity a zombie's regressive shuffling quickly improves and even their speech settles into something like a southern drawl. They've also taken to building small wooden temples and engaging in extended trance-like states following the consumption of coca leaves and various sweet-smelling herbs. 'God', 'spirit', 'beauty', and 'love' have replaced 'me', 'hungry', 'fuck now', and 'kill' in their limited vocabulary. Dr Bland has considered introducing his small tribe back into the modern world, but they appear extremely fearful of this possibility. Those breeding with the mountain men explained, with no apparent irony, that they have a great distrust of human violence. They have completely lost their appetite for human flesh, almost as though fearing some sort of moral contagion. When told that humans call them 'the walking dead', Dr Bland reports faint traces of humour. That, apparently, is what they now call us.

I'M TALKING MY WAY INTO A POEM AGAIN

and eventually, possibly out of it,
but I know from experience
there's more to this
than mere gossip and stiff verbs. I'm
hoping that something will come alive
like a breeze lifting a loved one's skirt,
or Dorothy's grey Kansas road
suddenly plunged into brilliant yellow.
And, of course, I'm writing this
for you (happy you've stumbled
onto this page) and for those
Michelangelo called 'the unseen witnesses'
who live in Plato's cave. Ends
and beginnings, comings and goings,
how they haunt our human story. I keep
thinking of all those homeless poems
crowding the borders, waiting to cross over
like an endless stream of refugees.

X-RAY

It's difficult not to be curious
about this bone-man under the skin,
to think how he's carried me over the years
without malice or contempt. In return
I've fed and clothed him of course,
shared the same bed, been shaped by his will,
but even after a lifetime together
I can't say I know him, not for real…
apart, that is, from a broken wrist
when he once came peeping through.
And now there's this inner-map of his ills,
that ageing stoop, those honeycombed hips,
the thinning tail-end bits. But what
really appals is his Model-T look.
He's indistinguishable – except to the nurse –
from the millions like him who've come and gone
since one of us first stood up. Perhaps
it's time to applaud his ancestral support
and keep this negative by the bed. Even then
it'll be tough to view that crumbling master-plan
without a more personal sense of loss.

PAVEMENTS

It's the way, looking down, they stick in the mind
'stained with time', dog crap, blood of course,
and 'things' that live in the cracks in spite
of clumsy juggernauts and the morning crowd.

Then there's the patterning – street after street
repeating themselves with hypnotic ease –
and certain abstract qualities…
sunlight on cobbles, shadows on stones.

But it's mostly the thought of 'the way made smooth'
by centuries of passing feet;
some sense of an earthly pilgrimage pursued
through circumstance rather than faith.

In any event, looking up, as one must
when coming to the edge of town,
I notice (with regret sometimes)
the strength with which barer elements rush in.

It's there, where pavements turn into hills,
that the lonely cult of destination…begins.

THE GENERAL

They came at night. Our neighbours. The ones we'd invited round for supper the previous evening. Only this time they were armed and led by a general from the city. At gunpoint he took us to the beautiful baroque hotel next to the railway station, tied a large pig to a marble pieta in the ballroom, and slit its throat. Then he did the same to our young men. Our women, of course, were raped. The rest of us were loaded onto buses – carefully monitored by international officials – and driven to the border.

That was years ago. Today we live in a snow-covered No Man's land between two countries. Or is it three? The guards keep changing their uniforms and their flags and moving the border posts. We hug the ever-changing but narrow strip of land between these disputed territories, struggling to keep ourselves in full view of the aid helicopters that sometimes get through with packets of aspirin and bundles of second-hand designer clothes. The worst things happen in the forest at night. We can hear the machine-guns and see the dark shapes of the soldiers tip-toeing into the pines.

The general visits us occasionally in his limousine, accompanied by well-dressed foreigners who ask us the usual questions. Are we being treated properly? Do we get enough food? The general watches and smiles, patting our children on the head and distributing small pieces of chocolate to the dying. When the foreign officials leave in their Land Rovers he waves them off. Then he shoots anyone who'd dared to complain. 'Soon,' he yells, 'when you are all under the earth, we will breathe untainted air!' This thought never fails to cheer him up. His men slap each other on the back and kick in a few of our heads. They drink a fiery liquid made of goat's blood and resin.

As each year passes we seem to be increasingly ignored. The guards are beginning to see us as part of the landscape. But, secretly, we are acquiring a history. With the coming of spring we plant a few vines on the barbed wire, trap rabbits and birds, and tend small patches of wild fruit. Wolves share our camp fires. Herbs and mushrooms thrive among the damp leaves. The Land Rovers are getting through more often. There's even talk of leasing us this strip of land. The general is looking tired. There are rumours he may be named as a war criminal, made a national hero, and asked to retire. In the meantime his wife wants him back in the city so that she can attend civic dinners and meet visiting pop stars. The general always has to remember that there were other generals before him and that younger fitter generals are waiting in the wings. His bodyguards are becoming increasingly nervous.

It will be a good harvest this year. We've planted some rice and dug irrigation ditches. Even the new lot of border guards are relaxing and throwing us the odd scrap of food. Our children have begun to play hide-and-seek in the ruins of last year's watch towers. We pray that, finally, we're beneath contempt.

THIS WAY TO SAMARKAND

Whenever I'm broke and grubbing around
for the price of a pint, I think
of James Elroy Flecker who wrote
anything to pay the bills –
tourist blurbs, trade journal guff –
writing it with a will and in
a white shirt because that way
he might get hired again. Not
a popular man (having no influence)
and a bit of a stay-at-home, but
in the few hours he won for himself
then to hell with bangers and mash and
yahoo to the local literati! Keeping
his head in the clouds he built
the entire city of Samarkand. No one
knocked on those doors with a bailiff.
And so, whenever I'm broke, I join
James Elroy on his elephant-clouds
heading east over the roofs of the town
with the sunlight streaming through our empty hands
and our wives and children swaying at the back.

ON GOVERNMENT LAWNS

Fat peasants hurl their Gucci bags
in the faces of the press. Country
cousins are new here. They'll soon learn.
Only last week they were dressed in rags
and crawling across parched fields. How
elegant the generals' wives are! And
the generals themselves are trying so hard
to be decent and well-bred. At least
one can't hear the screams in the palace yard
above the massed murmur of string quartets.
And the doves are lovely. (Except
for the dead ones.) Whole
container-trucks full of peace! On
government lawns past Presidents
are playing golf with some refugees.
How happy the old statesmen are
now that the assassins are somewhere else!
They wave their clubs and weep. In
a rush of patriotism at the champagne bar
two bodyguards shoot each other
through the knees. It's a farce of course –
but on such a scale! When the handshakes cease
bodies are piled up house-high in the streets.

SCARECROW

For my daughter

Your portable scarecrow
made from this and that
seems to attract
what he's supposed
to scare off. Sparrows
gather on his outstretched limbs
where falling feathers
turn his arms to wings. I suppose
he enjoys a certain poise
as your private garden god
or suburban Pan,
but what's he doing
guarding *one* potted plant
in the bare backyard
of your council flat?
Surely this is a case
of overkill? Each time
you move house
we watch amazed
at how adroitly
he settles in. Perhaps
he's the last of a dying race
hiding away among high-rise blocks?
Moths gather round
like ghosts at dusk
and snails cling to him
in warty heaps.

FLÂNEUR

> *Flânerie: an aimless reflective strolling that many city-dwelling poets prefer.*

These days there aren't many of us left.
We're hard to spot among the passing crowds,
the shoppers, joggers – always in a sweat –
the iPod and the cellphone lot
who never look up from their own quick thumbs
as passing breezes brush their limbs.
Best think of us as aimless hangers-on
without strict purpose or known destination.
You'll find us, should you care to look,
wandering back alleys and abandoned wharves
well away from the tourist traps. At
dusk we rest and cool parched tongues,
hoarding silences, talking to the dead,
recalling how a spent day came and went.

BEYOND

He was looking through the MIND, BODY, SPIRIT section of his local bookshop (a rather splendid place with easy chairs and a coffee shop) when he noticed a most intriguing scent…distant, evasive, faintly eastern (as most scents are) but – in essence –something 'other', something he'd never come across before. For a moment he distrusted himself and suspected a hidden joss-stick or the misty trace of some particularly subtle perfume warming itself on a passing wrist. But he was alone, leaning against ALIENS AND ANCHORITES, with no girlish hand nearby exploring those bookish depths. Further possibilities quickly presented themselves…a new brand of coffee…a Turkish cigarette…a sudden breeze from the flower-stall outside? None of these lived up to closer examination. Was this then the whiff of something alien or angelic? A ghostly longing that had somehow found a gathering place? A secret scented message from outer space? Do they have scents 'out there' in those deserts between the stars? In a flurry of belief that the answers to his questions lay hidden within those religious shelves, he began to unload their wisdom, a book at a time. *Poems for the Pope*, *A Day with the Dalai Lama*, *Secrets of the Incas*, were quickly piled up on a firm foundation of Korans and Holy Bibles. He felt like a child again, kneeling happily among his building blocks. But behind a large hardback edition of *Isis Unveiled*, that faint scent disappeared…crowded out, he felt, by the sheer weight of spiritual understanding that burdened those slender shelves. It was immediately replaced by the familiar odour of his own damp clothes. He had no regrets. What had been given was wholly of its moment. He sensed that if its origins *could* have been known, then they may well have turned out to be disturbingly matter-of-fact (like heat from the sun or the inevitability of oblivion). So it was back to the cappuccinos and the easy chairs, with an erotically illustrated volume of *The Song of Solomon* somehow left open on his lap. Shades of a post-war Sunday School and a disapproving vicar. Childhood intimations of close encounters with future perfumed unknowns.

WILDERNESS MOMENTS IN ORANGE COUNTY

For Beryl

Between the Taco stand and the Used-car lot
on Santa Clara, there's that single patch
of date-palms where green parrots come
squawking to their nests high-up
in those dried-out fronds. Such
wilderness moments, bordering the freeway,
relive themselves again and again
like the lone coyote
who kept strolling past Safeways
or that stranded whale among flustered sails
down at Marina-del-Rey. (Throw away
your Moby Dick!) But it's mainly
the memory of those birds returning
with both of us clinging to that ache at dusk;
the first stars gathering much as those birds do
but silently…and further off.

OVERHEARD IN MALIBU

Sir, as a visitor 'stunned' by our spaces,
desert silences, endless skies,
how *should* we populate vacancy – this
boredom brooding above the sprinklers,
these vast horizons at the end of the drive?

You note, in passing, that we build our homes
'in a plethora of imported styles' – Greek,
Roman, Elizabethan – all at odds
with our 'lack of roots', but you smile
at the burglar alarm's Mickey Mouse chimes.

And the light, you write, 'is like a glance from God.'
That's cute. We love your Gothic wit.
You Europeans are so *surrealist*...damn,
there's another coyote in the pool! You conclude
we're most at home when we stroll

'through the cool of endless shopping malls;'
that we live 'in suburbs like giant parking lots
sprawled on the edge of space...'
You see us as lapsed moralists
hiding behind our shades

avoiding that 'bright stare into nothingness'
that glitters above these waves
where, westward, the Pacific
(how well you put it)
'endlessly uncurls its nerveless blue.'

TRAVELLING WEST

i.m. Weldon Kees 1914–1955

We made love while the bombers roared on by.
– Weldon Kees

Death, jazz, motels, 'the spirit of the times!' –
your life was a plot from *Black Mask*. I'm trying to unwind
that condemned man's calm inside your head
that 'flapped like a worn-out blind', but get stuck
in such '50s detail: the motel clock,
cars like fish, the blackened seeds
that fell from your potted peony. Most of all
there's that Edward Hopper light…the air
full of vacancy, the street's
rouged glow. You knew
that the great trek westwards had run out
to the tune of an ad-man's jingle. (Vargas girls
flashing thighs on the sides
of Truman's bombers; Hughes and Ford
printing their dollars in some mad high-rise.) In
that rented room where you and Death played chess,
where 'a chilly landscape tightened up the mind'
I still see your piano, your artist's brush, stark
black-and-white photos from 'a used-up life.'
In the end you simply strolled outside
giving yourself to the tide,
drifting off from where the wagons stopped…
used-car lots blinking on the road behind.

HOMAGE TO HOPPER

The artist and his wife
on the move, seeking
America, that moveable feast
with its petrol stops,
cinemas, shops,
old brownstone blocks,
neat wooden towns. And
always and everywhere
that haunted look
of lives lived alone
even in a crowd…
the silent housewife,
the bored usherette,
the nude on the roof,
the dude with a fag.
Until, at the end
– his wife laid to rest –
there's an empty room
and absence itself
with a forest outside
looming dark and huge
and on the move
like the woods in *Macbeth*.

THE GOLDEN PARROTS OF ORANGE COUNTY

The desert parrots of Ponderosa
gather in gaunt rows, going nowhere.
They shriek at the sun,
scratch their own shadows
and nibble dead rats
in windy hollows.

But the golden parrots of Orange County
blessed with uncommon civic bounty
have ivory beaks
and silver talons
and peck petits pois
in botanical gardens.

SHOPPING WITH BRIGITTE BARDOT

Naturally one remembers you as you were. At
your best, I'd guess, in *Viva Maria*,
singing rebel songs and letting off bombs
in a Mexican bar with some footlights on
and lots of revolutionaries cheering. Footlights
suited you – Louis Malle knew that –
and frills and corsets and torn Edwardian knickers.
What we wouldn't have given, back in the '60s,
to share your bed…if only for a minute!
Now you're into dogs and stray goats
because 'they're always there' and 'never cheat me,'
not like those playboys in the bad old days
who whisked you away, knowing time was short
and that what they craved
could only be borrowed. Today
you've put on weight, got some wrinkles
round the eyes and throat, but it's still a pleasure
to watch you carry your dog food
back to the car, to admire your stride
and feel nostalgically voyeuristic. There's
the scent of Chanel and warm milk on your skin
and when you get home the dogs will start barking,
eager – like those playboys – to get you to themselves,
to lick you to death and cover you in kisses.

A COLD DAY IN ASSISI

For Brother Jonathan

A snowstorm in mid-May! It swept us
past Giotto's visual aids
towards that crypt-café where we ate
green gnocchi next to *another* dead nun. Outside
was that white church like a wedding-cake
built over Francis's stone hut. (Did
I sense soul-stirrings in that Platonic cave
or had my third grappa warmed
cold feelings up?) All day
we trudged through freezing alleyways
from tomb to tomb…coming, at last,
to that roof of lapis lazuli
where God's blind saint lies thirty feet
below the Etruscan light he loved. What
frenzy of grief or mad expediency
built, in weeks, a whole cathedral, dug
through granite, wrapped in iron straps
those frail bones, that poet's tongue.
Admit it, your happy warrior-turned-monk
had led us there through ice and mud
to beg for the coming of Brother Sun!
And it worked…after prayers
a gap in the clouds; birds
singing for our fallen crumbs. Thanks
for that grappa, and the warmth you shared
with a shivering stranger who spoke in tongues.

BARCELONA

Citizens so love this city
they find it difficult to leave
even in sleep…much of which
takes place in mid-afternoon
so that the noise, scents, torpor,
and diesel-filled light
of these late 19th century streets
enter not only their waking lives
but also their noon-day dreams:
some of which are about fish,
the harbour being full of them –
none healthy enough to eat
but all swimming blindly
in heart-rending spirals
with a sort of stunned
myopic grace. The beauty
of this ancient place
is everywhere and indisputable,
from the melting towers of the Sagrada Familia
to the white gorilla with a spoilt child's face
caged in the Ciutadella park
and visited on holidays and Sundays
by families who pose like Renoir paintings
among rows of manicured
civic trees. One should also mention
the Gaudi fountain, rarely working,
and the ice-cream carts with their big brass lids,
and the doves of course, Picasso loved them
as he did the fat geese on the cathedral pond
and the balconied-whores in the Gothic Quarter
with their faces like African masks. The Art
Gallery, the one in the park, for the city
is full of them, is dated but devoted
to a local over-the-top Art Nouveau
that brings us – there's no escape –
back to Gaudi (much loved

by Franco for his religious fervour).
The man is everywhere, breaking plates,
bending stones, moulding metal.
The scent of his lavender-tinted drains
lingers for miles out to sea. Dogs
leap from the decks of passing yachts
and swim in packs to reach these shimmering streets.

THE 1929 ESSEX SIX

Our first car, bought for a fiver
from a farmer who'd dumped it years before
under thick gorse in a corner paddock
where mushrooms sprouted on the back seat.
After days of tinkering we got it going,
double-declutching through the gears
as we loaded up for our move to the city
with children, dustbins, booze and poetry
before thundering south, shedding oil and steam.

On bad backroads, mud up to the bonnet,
pelted by hail and mountain floods,
that big cab ploughed down the whole north island
before shivering to a sudden stop
outside our state-house door. After that
we could never get it going. The canvas
roof shredded in an onshore wind,
tyres turned to mush, kids smashed the windscreen,
slugs browsed in herds across a mildewed floor.

We sold it off in bits: chrome headlamps,
wooden steering wheel, asthmatic horn.
An old Greek fisherman bought the engine block
for his crayfish boat. He was lost at sea.
I don't suppose even that's the end of it.
Under swaying kelp, some scenes – mostly those
full of journeys – float up in our dreams
along with the beat of that long-stroking Six,
when the road was a river beneath our feet.

– WELLINGTON, NEW ZEALAND

THE DESERTED BORDER

This deserted border
at the back of beyond
in a country whose name
I can't even pronounce
has become an oasis
of trees and streams
where broken barriers
sway like sails. For years
the maps have all been changed,
flags torn down, guards
dispersed. Old borders
such as this, once the scene
of blood-soaked crossings
and starving crowds
become, when forgotten
and gone to seed,
among the most peaceful spots
on earth, places
you'd picnic
on a summer's day
or even happily
put down roots.

DÉJÀ VU

We've passed this way
 several times before. How
often I can't truly say
– memory fades with age –
 but I recognize the tiny harbour
with its clutter of old boats
pulled ashore. And the locals
nod as if we're remembered
and they want us to know
there's a place for us here
should we call it home.
Yes, we've eaten before
at this neon-lit cafe
and the same table will be waiting
wherever we go, the same
moonlit graveyard overlooking
the sea, the same
lump in our throats
at arriving, or leaving
this stopping place, this pause
on the road, this small
corner of the earth
that we know we know.

Loss

in memory of my wife
Beryl Matilda Bland
1932–2009

No more journeys shared:
you've gone on alone.

Who do I turn to
in the deserts of dawn?

You were the keeper
of the campsite …

the madonna of the open road.

1. LOSS

I was telling you off
when you died. You'd tried
to get out of bed,
then fell. (You should
have rung the bell.) I was
angry lifting you up,
bullying death to the end.
It was then you took
your last breath. I saw
a mist leave your head.
I tried to bring
you back. I cried out
'What have I done?' But
you'd put a border
between us, a distance
no one could cross. I knew
it wasn't you on the bed.
What was left could never
be soothed with a kiss
or rise up and sing us
a song. This was loss. It
would take your place
from now on. It was
an absence I had to live.

2. ANGRY

Those final months
were full of pain.
Pills, patches, needles,
nothing worked. You asked me
what you'd done that God
should put you through this
for so long … and you
tried really hard
to think of something.
I was angry with God,
with the absent nurse,
and anyone else
who should have been there
as you sank into yourself.
I lost you slowly,
breath by breath. We
were almost strangers
by the time you left.

3. OUTRAGE

I refuse to look
at what death
has done to her. This
is not the woman
I loved. Close
the lid! What you
have here is an outrage.
Do with it what you will!

4. CLEARING OUT

Your clothes first, already bagged
for burning. Charity shops
are too risky. I couldn't bear
the shock of seeing some stranger
wearing your worn-out jeans. Jewellery
next. Nothing serious there. I'll
distribute it to the kids
(average age almost fifty).
The rest, as they say, is silence.
Your body follows, then mine (in time)
then our children, then our children's
children, then the earth itself
(because everything passes) and
none of this is closer to my heart
than your bus-pass, passport, old
driving licence. All of which
I put carefully to one side.

5. HABITS OF A LIFETIME

The little things I took for granted
keep coming back now you're not here.

I loved to watch you dress in the morning
and make yourself ready for the day.

Out shopping you'd drag me into Marks
for trousers. You knew

my size by heart. By the way
that winter coat you ordered for me,

secretly, knowing you'd not be here,
was timed my darling to perfection …

delivered the day the first snow arrived.

6. FUGUE

Today a fugue by Bach is playing
everywhere you used to be:
in my head, the street,
the spice aisle at Sainsbury's,
the car, down
on the beach.
          For a moment
I'm holding you close again,
warm lips, soft skin,
little feet sculptured by Bellini,
breasts that thrill.
            Now Bach's
moving heavenwards as only he can
and I'm listening for the two of us,
begging a lift.

7. THE PIANO

Of course, being dead, you're everywhere. It's
to be expected but still a shock
when I swear I can hear you playing Purcell
on that battered upright you bought for a song
more than a lifetime ago. Today
I found your scrawl on the phone-pad
as fresh as if you'd left it there
while I'd slipped out of the room. You were
making arrangements to style your hair. By
then it must have grown back. Your
photo at sixty in a slinky dress
reminds me that age didn't wither you
although that last long illness did. Now
the clichés begin to mount up: 'Time
heals' … 'Love conquers death' … 'She's
gone ahead.' I believe them all
but the piano has to go. My one-
fingered *Chopsticks*, hopelessly forlorn,
breaks down with an ache for your lost baroque.

8. TRINKETS

Two keyboard pieces, early
18th century. A rondeau
and a minuet. 'Trinkets'
you called them. I'm
obsessed by their delicacy
(and yours in my memory)
playing them over
and over again. Trinkets
are like that. They echo
the essence of grave-goods
as do your glass beads,
ivory comb, gold ring,
and these old tunes
that you played so well,
with lightness and just
a touch of melancholy
(but for the music
and not yourself).
Two trinkets then
(possibly by Couperin)
a rondeau and a minuet.

9. ELEMENTAL

I'm sitting, my love, where we always sat,
on a shingle-bank overlooking the sea.
No one, you said, *can outstare
the ocean.* We often tried,
for hours on end. I'm still
collecting the small black pebbles
and pearly-white shells you neatly placed
in Taoist circles on the kitchen shelf.
Your best bone-china smells of seaweed.
Love's elemental, made of salt and sand
and an earthly fire that still smoulders
and staring out at what stares blindly back.

10. OTHER TIMES, OTHER PLACES

Here's a sun-bleached photo from the 1930s
of children playing on an Auckland beach.
You're the pretty one with the sun in your face.
(Even this far away my eyes are hurting.) So
there you are in your soggy togs
and I can't see Death
anywhere near you. I feel
like shouting *Don't walk this way!*
And this is before you were you, before
we shared a lifetime together. (I'm
probably toddling on a colder beach
half a world away
and not even waving.) We're
star-crossed lovers and you're barely four
and I'm staring across the distance between us.

11. LETTING LIGHT IN

I'm admiring those panels
of old stained glass
you fitted yourself
to our dull front door.
Edwardian abstracts
of green and gold
whose crystal lozenges
and gloopy spirals
give the winter sun
a summery sheen. You
loved where light gathers,
lit candles, hearth-fires,
and now I recall
your bright shy smile
when that glass came alive
and torrents of light
first plunged
through the porch
and flooded the hall.

12. I'LL BE WAITING

outside the Turkish Café
on Victoria Street. The one
with the belly dancer
and the honey cakes
and a sweet pungent scent
of the East. I'll be there
every evening at 6
just in case you can make it
down to earth. Wear
that blue slinky dress,
the one with gold beads
that move when you do. It
makes me feel so alive!
I'll be there early. I want
to watch you arrive. I want
to feel my heart skip
as you stroll through
the crowd. Remember
at 6, outside the Turkish Café
in that blue slinky dress
that catches the light.

13. POPPIES

The poppy seeds you gathered from the park
and sprinkled in our small backyard
have flowered from every cranny
in the wall, through flagstones,
concrete, long-abandoned pots,
adding splashes of pink and scarlet
to a dull jungle of muddy weeds.
Like your bright dresses when you struggled
to hang them out in the morning breeze
they give the day a sunlit flutter
and fill my heart with such a flounce.

14. COLD

Your death was in mid-winter.
My fingers froze
to your coffin lid. One
year on and they say it's colder
than '46 when the Thames
froze over. Not true
but it is the same deep chill
as the day my mother died
or my drowned sea-brother
(both mid-winter
wartime deaths). Something
froze in me before I met you.
Global warming couldn't ease
that chill. You did. When
I fed you cubes of ice you smiled
as they melted on cracked lips.

15. ASHES

It's not that I can't let them go
but no one place claims you.
Take your pick. I could
pour you out under Putney Bridge,
drop you off from Worthing Pier,
or scatter you on that Auckland hill
where you grew up, pretending
to be a white horse. In time
I could join you: twin urns passed down
the family line from year to year
until some distant stranger slyly
dumps us at a wayside station
or spills us into a waiting wind.

16. CLICK

More photos of small boats
on the beach. I can't resist
their shape. (Each is
so utterly itself.) Click!
That's you with your back
to the sun. You've got
a halo and you're looking
sacred. Don't worry,
just because you're dead
doesn't mean I've lost it. I'm
merely creating selected vacancies
of time and place
where you might have been
had you not wandered out of frame
and walked a little ahead.

17. STALKER

I remember how
when you woke early
dawn followed you
about the house
aroused by the landscapes
behind your eyes
and the music and light
that clothed your body.

Now that you've gone
the dawn feels lonely.
It doesn't know
what to do with itself.
It searches the mirrors
where you came and went
but gets lost in the depths
of their emptiness.

18. DIDN'T I SAY?

Didn't I say how much I loved you?
Didn't I *know* how much I cared?
Didn't I beg you to come closer?
Didn't I try to ease the pain?

I'd like to think it was all bad timing
but what I recall was your quiet grace
and the fear I suddenly put between us
when death arrived to take my place.

19. THERE YOU ARE

Last night in a dream I was trying to find you. We'd been told on TV that the world was coming to an end, but you were far away by the sea. What were you doing there? I needed you. Didn't you care enough to be close by? I hitched a lift. I caught a train. I boarded a boat. I hijacked a plane. I walked for miles through deserted streets in several countries both known and unknown. Finally I tracked you down. You were one of the crowd in a sort of holiday camp but, suddenly, I saw you. I was so full of need and anxiety I couldn't speak. You were wearing jeans and a summery blouse and you looked lovely. You seemed to be packing something. Anyway, you were busy. I quickly forgot that it was the end of the world. I wanted to hug you but there were so many people milling about and you didn't seem interested. I was always hugging you and sometimes you found it embarrassing. It was the way you were brought up. Now I'd found you I wanted to take you away. Why didn't I? Why didn't we speak? Perhaps you didn't know I was there? Then I woke up. I always wake up before the end of the world, or before you look at me. It doesn't matter. I'd found you. That was the main thing. Can I please have that dream repeated. Can it be put on a loop and played over and over again. Please wear the same jeans and blouse so I can get to know the exact details of every move you make. You don't have to say anything. Just be there like you always were. What's fifty years together? It's barely a beginning. Please let me find you again. Sooner or later I promise I'll get to know you better. One day, I know you'll look up.